PHILIPPIANS

8 STUDIES FOR INDIVIDUALS AND GROUPS

N. T. WRIGHT

WITH DALE & SANDY LARSEN

IVP Connect

An imprint of InterVarsity Press
Downers Grove, Illinois

InterVarsity Press
P.O. Box 1400, Downers Grove, IL 60515-1426
World Wide Web: www.ivpress.com
E-mail: email@ivpress.com

InterVarsity Press® is the book-publishing division of InterVarsity Christian Fellowship/USA®, a
movement of students and faculty active on campus at hundreds of universities, colleges and schools
of nursing in the United States of America, and a member movement of the International Fellowship of
Evangelical Students. For information about local and regional activities, write Public Relations Dept.,
InterVarsity Christian Fellowship/USA, 6400 Schroeder Rd., P.O. Box 7895, Madison, WI 53707-7895, or
visit the IVCF website at <www.intervarsity.org>.

Cover design: Cindy Kiple
Cover image: Andy & Michelle Kerry/Trevillion Images
Interior image: Clipart.com

ISBN 978-0-8308-2191-4

Printed in the United States of America ∞

P	19	18	17	16	15	14	13	12	11	10
Y	25	24	23	22	21	20	19	18		

CONTENTS

GETTING THE MOST OUT
OF PHILIPPIANS

Philippi, in northern Greece, was the first place in Europe that heard the news that there was a new king, the crucified and risen Jesus of Nazareth. You can read the story of Paul's first visit there in Acts 16. This letter makes it clear that as Paul looked at all the churches he had founded, the people of Philippi were the ones who gave him the most joy. He loved them all, but this letter breathes a confident trust and enjoyment which we don't always find elsewhere.

For Paul, bringing the gospel to Greece (described in Acts 16:9-12) was like a completely new beginning (see Philippians 4:15). Although he had been preaching and planting churches in Asia Minor (modern Turkey) for some while, he seems to have had a sense that when he came in to Europe he really was in new territory, and that if the gospel took root here it would prove in a further sense just how powerful it was. These, after all, were the Macedonians and Greeks, who had given the world one of its greatest cultures to date! And the Philippian church was the first of those churches on Greek soil.

Philippi was a Roman colony. In 42 B.C., about a hundred years before Paul came to that area, Philippi was the setting for one of the great battles in the Roman civil war that had broken out after the death of Julius Caesar. The two victorious generals, Antony and Octavian (the future Emperor Augustus), had found themselves with a lot of soldiers in northern Greece with nothing more to do. They certainly didn't want to bring them all back to Rome, or even to Italy. It would be dangerous to have thousands of soldiers suddenly arriving in the capital. So they gave them land in and around Philippi, making it a colony of Rome.

Once the colony was established, other veterans from other battles joined them. By the time Paul went there, Philippi contained quite a number of families descended from those original Roman colonists, as well as several local people who had benefited from the Roman presence—and a good many who hadn't, and who resented the Latin-speaking elite that had taken over their Greek town.

Philippi was on a main road which ran west to the narrowest part of the Adriatic Sea, where you could sail easily across to Italy and travel on to Rome. Close contact could be maintained with the mother city. The Philippian colonists were proud of being Romans, and would do their best to order their civic life so that it matched the way things were done in Rome. The most recent innovation down that line was, of course, the establishment of the imperial cult: Caesar, the emperor, was to be worshiped as savior and lord.

Now, some time after the church had been established, Paul is in prison, almost certainly in Ephesus since he speaks of coming to see them again (1:26), and in his other imprisonments he had no intention of returning to Greece. When people were put in prison in Paul's world, they were not normally given food by their captors; they had to rely on friends helping them. The Philippian Christians have sent Paul a gift of money, presumably a quite substantial gift, since it would hardly have been worthwhile sending a messenger with a small amount. One of the reasons Paul writes to them is to say a heartfelt "Thank you." (For more on this letter also see my *Paul for Everyone: The Prison Letters,* on which this guide is based, published by SPCK and Westminster John Knox.)

The fact that people from a different country would raise money, and send one of their number (Epaphroditus, see 4:18) on the dangerous journey to carry it to an imprisoned friend, speaks volumes for the esteem and love in which they held him. People sometimes speak today as though Paul was an awkward, difficult, unpopular sort of person, but folk like that don't normally find this kind of support reaching them unbidden from friends far away.

Paul's own circumstances make this letter especially poignant, and it gives us a portrait of a man facing huge difficulties and hardships, and coming through with his faith and hope unscathed. We will see through this guide, prepared with the help of Dale and Sandy Larsen for which I am grateful, what he has to say to this young church. Already, within thirty years of Jesus' death and resurrection, Paul has worked out a wonderful, many-colored picture of what Jesus achieved, of God's worldwide plan and of how it all works out in the lives of ordinary people.

SUGGESTIONS FOR INDIVIDUAL STUDY

1. As you begin each study, pray that God will speak to you through his Word.

2. Read the introduction to the study and respond to the "Open" question that follows it. This is designed to help you get into the theme of the study.

3. Read and reread the Bible passage to be studied. Each study is designed to help you consider the meaning of the passage in its context. The commentary and questions in this guide are based on my own translation of each passage found in the companion volume to this guide in the For Everyone series on the New Testament (published by SPCK and Westminster John Knox).

4. Write your answers to the questions in the spaces provided or in a personal journal. Each study includes three types of questions: observation questions, which ask about the basic facts in the passage; interpretation questions, which delve into the meaning of the passage; and application questions, which help you discover the implications of the text for growing in Christ. Writing out your responses can bring clarity and deeper understanding of yourself and of God's Word.

5. Each session features selected comments from the For Everyone series. These notes provide further biblical and cultural background and contextual information. They are designed not to answer the questions for you but to help you along as you study the Bible for yourself. For even more reflections on each passage, you may wish to have on hand a copy of the companion volume from the For Everyone series as you work through this study guide.

6. Use the guidelines in the "Pray" section to focus on God, thanking him for what you have learned and praying about the applications that have come to mind.

SUGGESTIONS FOR GROUP MEMBERS

1. Come to the study prepared. Follow the suggestions for individual study mentioned above. You will find that careful preparation will greatly enrich your time spent in group discussion.

2. Be willing to participate in the discussion. The leader of your group will not be lecturing. Instead, she or he will be asking the questions found in this guide and encouraging the members of the group to discuss what they have learned.

3. Stick to the topic being discussed. These studies focus on a particular passage of Scripture. Only rarely should you refer to other portions of the Bible or outside sources. This allows for everyone to participate on equal ground and for in-depth study.

4. Be sensitive to the other members of the group. Listen attentively when they describe what they have learned. You may be surprised by their insights! Each question assumes a variety of answers. Many questions do not have "right" answers, particularly questions that aim at meaning or application. Instead the questions push us to explore the passage more thoroughly.

   When possible, link what you say to the comments of others. Also, be affirming whenever you can. This will encourage some of the more hesitant members of the group to participate.

5. Be careful not to dominate the discussion. We are sometimes so eager to express our thoughts that we leave too little opportunity for others to respond. By all means participate! But allow others to also.

6. Expect God to teach you through the passage being discussed and through the other members of the group. Pray that you will have an enjoyable and profitable time together, but also that as a result of the study you will find ways that you can take action individually and/ or as a group.

7. It will be helpful for groups to follow a few basic guidelines. These guidelines, which you may wish to adapt to your situation, should be read at the beginning of the first session.

   • Anything said in the group is considered confidential and will not be discussed outside the group unless specific permission is given to do so.

   • We will provide time for each person present to talk if he or she feels comfortable doing so.

   • We will talk about ourselves and our own situations, avoiding conversation about other people.

   • We will listen attentively to each other.

   • We will be very cautious about giving advice.

Additional suggestions for the group leader can be found at the back of the guide.

1

Paul's Reasons for Thanks

Philippians 1:1-11

There's a wonderful old prayer attributed to the sixteenth-century sailor Sir Francis Drake (1540-1596). He prays that when God leads us to undertake any great piece of work, he will also remind us "that it is not the beginning, but the continuing of the same, until it be thoroughly finished, that yieldeth the true glory." Drake himself was certainly a "finisher" as well as a "beginner." As well as being a legend in his own lifetime for his military exploits, he had sailed right round the world. Once you've set off on a journey like that, there's no point stopping halfway.

OPEN

What are some examples you've seen that bear out this principle that there is more glory in finishing than beginning?

STUDY

1. *Read Philippians 1:1-11.* In this opening to his letter, what convictions does Paul express?

2. Why did the Philippians bring Paul joy?

3. Who is someone of whom you can say "I thank my God every time I think of you" (v. 3), and why?

4. This letter is all about *partnership* (v. 5), one of the most important words in Paul's vocabulary. It is sometimes translated *fellowship*, but it clearly has a practical, even financial, implication which our word *fellowship* doesn't always carry. Although it develops particular Christian meanings, including the delighted sharing of worship, prayer, and mutual support and friendship, in Paul's world it was the normal word for a business partnership, in which all those involved would share in doing the work on the one hand and in the financial responsibilities on the other.

   How had the Philippians worked in partnership with Paul?

5. Consider the Christian community you are part of. Would you say that you are in partnership for the gospel, or is your fellowship more social? Why do you answer as you do?

6. As Sir Francis Drake reminded us in his prayer, the glory is not in beginning a great task but in finishing it. The confidence Paul has throughout this letter is that God himself is a *finisher* as well as a *beginner* (v. 6). The particular work which God has begun, and will

finish, is the work of grace, through the gospel, in the hearts and lives of the Philippian Christians.

How is it easy or hard for you to trust God to complete the work he's started in you or in others? And why?

7. Paul prays that the Philippians' love will overflow in knowledge and wisdom (v. 9). How does this idea contrast with more popular ideas of love?

8. Paul also prays that this wise love will result in moral discernment (v. 10). Why is moral discernment a necessary component of Christian love?

9. Finally Paul prays that the Philippians may be filled to overflowing with the fruit of right living (v. 11). The word for *right living* is often translated *righteousness*. Here it emphasizes the behavior which results from both God's faithfulness and the status of being forgiven family members. What are some of the fruits of right living?

At every stage of the process—when people first hear the gospel, when they believe it, when they begin to live by it, and when they make progress in faith and love—nothing is done to the glory of the people concerned, as though they were able arrogantly to advance their own cause. Everything is done, as Paul insists here, through King Jesus, "to God's glory and praise" (v. 11).

10. Despite being in prison (v. 7), Paul begins his letter with an overflow of joy. How and why do you experience joy in your Christian life?

PRAY

Paul's prayer for the church (vv. 9-11) is a prayer that all church leaders might wish to use for the people in their care. It is also a prayer that every Christian might use for himself or herself. For yourself and for others, pray that all of you will have love which overflows in knowledge and wisdom, the ability to discern right from wrong, and the fruit of right living to the glory of God.

FULL OF HOPE

Philippians 1:12-26

As he writes the letter to the Philippians, Paul is faced with two problems, one on top of the other. In both cases he declares that what looks like a major difficulty is being turned by God into an opportunity for the gospel. The first part of the problem is that he's in prison. For a traveling apostle to be put in prison must have seemed like a concert pianist having his hands tied behind his back. The second problem is that there are people going around talking about King Jesus who don't really mean it. They don't believe the message; they merely want to make more trouble for him in his imprisonment. Paul, with his strong belief in the way God works through unlikely circumstances, is ready with an answer.

OPEN

When have you been faced with seemingly insurmountable problems, and seen God work good out of them? How did the experience(s) affect your faith?

STUDY

1. *Read Philippians 1:12-18.* How would you describe Paul's mood throughout this passage?

2. In what ways had Paul's imprisonment helped the gospel on its way (vv. 12-14)?

Every major center of Roman influence had an Imperial Guard, as was the case in Ephesus where Paul was likely imprisoned. The soldiers were used to the "gospel" of Caesar, the supposed good news that a new emperor had taken the throne, bringing (so he claimed) peace and justice to the world. Now here was someone announcing that there was a different gospel: that Jesus of Nazareth had taken the throne of the world and was summoning every person to bow the knee to him.

3. Considering the very real threat of prison, why then did Paul's imprisonment have such a positive effect on the Christians in Ephesus?

4. We are not exactly sure who Paul meant by those who preached Christ out of selfish ambition, without meaning it, trying to stir up trouble for him (v. 15). Some think these people were a rival Christian group. It seems more likely they were ordinary pagans who are talking up the latest piece of news. "Have you heard?" they'd say to each other. "They've caught that strange fellow Paul who's been going around saying there's a new king—a new emperor! And you won't believe it—this new king turns out to be a Jew they crucified a few

years ago, and this jailbird is saying he's alive again and he's the real Lord of the world! What a dangerous lunatic this Paul character is!"

What are some ways that Christ could be proclaimed out of "envy and rivalry" these days?

5. Consider Paul's response to the insincere teachers (v. 18). How can we apply the spirit of his response to those who talk about Jesus today, even for the wrong reasons?

6. How were the Philippians likely to feel knowing that Paul was in prison in Ephesus?

7. How would his words here comfort and encourage them?

Paul writes to encourage the church in Philippi, but his words ought also to be a great encouragement to us. How often are we tempted to feel discouraged because our plans were badly thwarted or because malicious people were trying to make life difficult? We need to learn from Paul the art of seeing God's purposes working out through problems and difficulties.

8. *Read Philippians 1:18-26.* Paul struggles with whether it would be better to die in custody or to be released and live. In either outcome, death or life, what are the advantages to Paul?

9. How would his comments help the Philippian Christians deal with their worries about Paul?

10. Paul feels confident that God has more work for him to do (vv. 23-25), even though he admits that his first desire is to be with God. How can his attitude here serve as a model for us in times of waiting?

Paul agrees that he would be better off dead. This is not a death wish in the sense of someone losing self-esteem, becoming terminally depressed and longing to get out of this life as quickly as possible. Paul is full of life and energy and quite ready to get back to work the minute they let him out of prison. But Paul is also a man in love with the Messiah. The central thing about dying is that it will mean going to be with Jesus, his lord, master and king. This language is perhaps the best and safest Christian way of talking about life after death since seldom in the New Testament do we find people talking about something like "going to heaven when I die." For Paul, as for most Jews, as we shall see in Philippians 3, the resurrection is still to come. The dead will receive new bodies to live in the new world that God will then make.

11. Paul's *belief* never wavered, indeed it came through the terrible experience strengthened (see 2 Corinthians 1:8-11). But his *feelings* came and went. Learning to distinguish between the two is itself part of Christian maturity. What is one circumstance right now in which you need to maintain your belief and hope in the midst of troubling feelings?

12. What are some circumstances in your life in which God has proved himself faithful regardless of how you felt?

PRAY

Bring your toughest problems to the Lord, and after you have named them, ask God to help you wait eagerly and full of hope because nothing is going to put you to shame (Philippians 1:20).

3

UNITY IN CHRIST

Philippians 1:27—2:4

From the first-century Mediterranean world to the twenty-first century in China, in the Sudan and in many other places, there have been plenty of people determined to stamp out this Christian nonsense and to use every trick in the book to do so. In the post-Christian West today, the forces of skepticism and cynicism within our culture are extremely powerful, not least in newspapers and on television. It's easy for Christians to feel intimidated; but Paul insists that we mustn't.

OPEN

Where and how have you experienced resistance to your faith? How did you feel? How did you respond?

STUDY

1. *Read Philippians 1:27—2:4.* Why is it important for Christians' public behavior to match up with the gospel?

2. What would be some examples of behavior which does and does not match up with the gospel?

3. Paul urges the Philippians to stand firm "with a single spirit, struggling side by side with one united intent for the faith of the gospel" (1:27). The aim is not unity for the sake of unity, because people can stand united for evil purposes. In your experience what is unique about the unity of Christians?

4. If we refuse to be intimidated by our opponents, what will be the result (1:28)?

5. What could the Philippians learn from Paul's example (1:29-30)?

6. Regarding what gospel issue does your community need to hold its nerve and remain unafraid in the face of resistance?

Appropriate public behavior and united work for the gospel will together send a signal to opponents: we're not afraid. And that signal is itself part of the gospel message. It functions as a sign to the Christians that they already belong to the coming king, and to their opponents that a new world is beginning in which the threats of the old one don't work any more.

7. How does the comfort and encouragement that comes from unity motivate us toward unity with each other in Christ (2:1)?

8. Paul doesn't say we should bring our thinking in line with each other. What instead is to be the center around which Christians unite?

9. Christians have theological differences, smoldering resentments from events of long ago, radical variations of styles of worship, personality cults, clashes over leadership style and arguments on issues of moral behavior. How can you and your Christian community work lovingly to overcome tensions like these with fellow Christians?

10. What are some practical ways to regard others as more important than you are (2:3)?

11. How can you look after someone else's best interests this week
    (2:4)?

PRAY

Pray for unity among believers, centered on the love of Christ. Pray especially about specific cases of disunity which you know about. Ask the Lord what you could do to help bring reconciliation.

4

THE MIND OF THE MESSIAH

Philippians 2:5-18

Whenen people in the ancient world thought of heroic leaders, rulers and kings they often thought of Alexander the Great (356-323 B.C.). At the age of twenty he succeeded his father to the throne of Macedonia, quickly made himself master of all Greece and then set about the task of conquering the rest of the world. By the time he died just shy of age thirty-three, he had succeeded to such an extent that it made sense for him to be regarded as divine.

In Paul's world the closest equivalent to Alexander was the emperor Augustus, who had put an end to the long-running Roman civil war and had brought peace to the whole known world. It wasn't long before many grateful subjects came to regard him, too, as divine. Only when we grasp this do we see just how deeply subversive, how utterly countercultural, was Paul's gospel message concerning Jesus of Nazareth, whose resurrection had declared him to be Israel's Messiah and the world's true Lord.

OPEN

Think about good leaders you have known as well as figures from history. What are the marks of an effective leader?

STUDY

1. There are some things that can perhaps only be said in poetry. While some translations don't lay out this passage as poetry, it is clearly a powerful poetic presentation of central Christian truth. *Read Philippians 2:5-11.* People still debate whether Paul wrote the poem himself or was quoting an even earlier Christian writer. In either case we have here a very, very early statement of Christian faith in who Jesus was and is and what he accomplished.

   In what ways did Jesus humble himself (vv. 6-8)?

2. How is Jesus now exalted (vv. 9-11)?

3. What is the connection between these two parts? Why should the Jesus who did what verses 6-8 say he did be honored in this way?

4. Compare the attitude of Christ in this passage with the typical attitude of worldly leaders.

5. How does your perspective on the world change when you consider that *every knee* shall bow and *every tongue* confess that Jesus is Lord (vv. 10-11)?

6. How does this poem fit with and emphasize what Paul said in the first part of Philippians 2?

7. *Read Philippians 2:12-18.* How does verse 13 make clear that the phrase "your own salvation" (v. 12) isn't meant to contrast the work of the Philippians with God's work?

8. Whose work then is being contrasted with that of the Philippians?

9. When Paul uses the phrase "fear and trembling," as it is often translated in verse 12, he means with "utter seriousness." What would it mean for you to work out the practical implications of your salvation in this way?

Paul is telling the Philippians that they must grow into maturity and take responsibility for themselves. Paul isn't there, and for all either of them know he may never be there again. He wants them to work out for themselves (on their own without him, but not without God) what this business of being saved will mean in practice. He stresses that the work of salvation is God's work from start to finish.

10. Verse 14 offers what appears to be a simple command. How would the lives of churches be revolutionized if Christians lived by this?

11. When Paul speaks of them shining like lights (v. 15) he is quoting a passage from the book of Daniel (12:3) which speaks of "the wise"—meaning Israelites skilled in knowing and applying God's law, not least in a time of persecution. Who comes to mind as examples of such lights?

12. The passage ends on a note of celebration (vv. 17-18). What gives Paul cause to celebrate?

13. Whose faith can you celebrate today?

PRAY

Thank the Lord Jesus for humbling himself for you, even to death on the cross. Praise him that every knee will bow to him and every tongue confess that he is Lord. Pray that you will shine as a bright light in a sin-darkened world.

NOTE ON PHILIPPIANS 2:6-7

In verse 7 Paul says that Jesus emptied himself. People have sometimes thought that this means that Jesus, having been divine up to that point, somehow stopped being divine and became human, and then went back to being divine again. This is, in fact, completely untrue to what Paul has in mind. The point of verse 6 is that Jesus was indeed already equal with God; somehow Paul is saying that Jesus already existed even before he became human (v. 7). But the decision to become human, and to go all the way along the road of obedience to the divine plan of salvation, all the way to the cross—this decision was not a decision to stop being divine. It was a decision about what it really meant to be divine. Jesus retained his equality with God. The eternal Son of God, the one who became human in and as Jesus of Nazareth, regarded his equality with God as committing him to the course he took. This is the true meaning of who God is. He is the God of self-giving love.

5

TIMOTHY AND EPAPHRODITUS

Philippians 2:19-30

If all Paul's writing was solid, dense, abstract theology we would never know what he was really like as a human being. We might have the idea that Paul lived the kind of Christian life one imagines from some popular literature: a life without stress or strain, a life of pure unmitigated joy and gladness, cheerfully doing the work of the Lord and preaching the gospel without a care in the world. This passage about Timothy and Epaphroditus helps us get Paul and his work—and his feelings and emotions—in true perspective.

OPEN

How are Christian friendships different from other friendships?

STUDY

1. *Read Philippians 2:19-30.* What qualities do Timothy and Epaphroditus share?

2. How is Timothy different from others Paul has worked with (vv. 20-21)?

3. Have you experienced or known of a relationship like that of Paul and Timothy (v. 22)? What was it like?

4. How does Paul indicate his profound trust in Timothy?

5. What is the connection between looking after the interests of others (2:4) and looking after the interests of Jesus the Messiah (v. 21)?

It is interesting that Paul doesn't say "Timothy is a wonderful teacher" or even "Timothy is a very devout and holy man," but "Timothy will genuinely care about you." The definition Paul seems to be adopting for a good pastor—and the implication is that he himself was like this—has more to do with sheer unselfish love than any other traits about the person.

6. Epaphroditus had carried the Philippians' gift to Paul (as we will see in Philippians 4:18). What had then happened which caused anxiety for everyone involved (vv. 25-27)?

7. How does Paul show his own vulnerability to the Philippians in verses 25-27?

8. Paul expresses thanks that Epaphroditus recovered, sparing him from having "one sorrow piled on top of another" (v. 27). How do you respond to the idea that Paul would have been stricken with sorrow if Epaphroditus had died?

9. How does Paul demonstrate that he was looking after the Philippians' interests and not only his own (vv. 28-30)?

Paul's description of Epaphroditus reminds us of the vital truth that we are all of us, whether first-century apostles or twenty-first-century converts, expected to be fully human beings, facing all that life throws at us and being honest about the results. Paul didn't need or want to hide from the young church, from his own converts. He was not afraid to admit to his own troubles.

10. Who has been a Timothy or an Epaphroditus in your life? In what ways?

11. Paul urges the Philippians to hold people like Epaphroditus "in special respect" (v. 29). How can you and/or your church do more to honor people who serve like Epaphroditus and Timothy?

PRAY

Thank God for partnerships in the gospel. Thank him specifically for the people with whom you serve and have served in even the simplest and seemingly insignificant ways. Ask God to show you someone you should bring alongside with you, or whom you should come alongside, to work in partnership.

NOTE ON PHILIPPIANS 2:27

Paul was grateful he didn't have one sorrow piled on another. The second would have been the death of Epaphroditus. The first presumably was being in prison and being unable to see his brothers and sisters in the Lord. Do these sorrows negate what he has said (and will say) in this letter about rejoicing? No, it makes clear that the joy Paul speaks of is not a call to ignore or forget the multiple human dimensions of our daily lives. After all, part of Jesus' own path of humble obedience (2:6-8) was weeping in agony both at his friend's graveside (John 11:35) and in Gethsemane (Hebrews 5:7).

The Worth of the King

Philippians 3:1-16

Ancestry and all that went with it was very important in the ancient world, as it is in many societies in our own day. Jews of the first century, who could trace their ancestry back for two thousand years to the patriarchs Abraham, Isaac and Jacob, and who knew which of Jacob's twelve sons they were descended from—such people were understandably and justifiably proud.

OPEN

What are some things you have treasured or benefited from? Consider not only physical objects but also achievements, honors and privileges.

STUDY

1. *Read Philippians 3:1-6.* This section and the second half of the letter is introduced by verse 1, which sometimes seems a little cut off from

what follows it. What is the connection between "celebrate in the Lord!" and the warnings which follow?

2. The badge of family, ethnic membership for the male Jew was circumcision, a mark on the physical body. Paul sees some of his contemporaries obsessed with this, particularly with inflicting it on Gentiles to try to make them acceptable to God. By contrast, who are the true "circumcision" (v. 3)?

3. Paul names various credits which once gave him reason to trust in the flesh (vv. 4-6). The main thing Paul meant by *the flesh* here (and often in Galatians and Romans) is the pride of *physical descent* cherished by the Jews. As this passage makes clear, he knew all about it from the inside. This had been his pride too. If you emphasized the "flesh" and your identity "according to the flesh," as he himself had done in his pre-Christian days, then instead of stressing something that made you different from the pagan world around, you were instead stressing that which you had in common with them. You were setting up your Judaism as just another ethnic, geographical, religious and cultural grouping, along with all the other ones in the world.

What are some accomplishments or aspects of religious or personal heritage that we use to make ourselves acceptable?

4. *Read Philippians 3:7-11.* What were Paul's "profit" and "loss"?

5. How do you respond to Paul's statement that "knowing King Jesus as my Lord is worth far more than everything else put together" (v. 8)?

Paul's accounts balance in a very odd way. He has just declared that in terms of his status as a member of God's people, Israel, he had nothing on the debit side at all. But he strikes a line through all the items that looked as though they had formed a credit balance and places the whole lot on the debit side of the page instead. Paul has discovered something to put on the credit side in comparison with which everything else can only be a debit. That something is of course some*one*, Jesus the Messiah, through whose faithfulness to the point of death we are declared right with God. No matter who our parents were or what their moral, cultural or religious background may have been. Our belief that the crucified and risen Jesus is the Messiah, the Lord of the world, and our loyalty to him, are the sign and badge that we have a credit balance consisting simply of him, over against all the debits we could ever have from anywhere else. This is Paul's famous doctrine of *justification by faith* which continues to be a comfort and a challenge to millions around the world.

6. What relationship does Paul draw between resurrection and suffering (vv. 10-11)?

7. *Read Philippians 3:12-16.* What is the goal of Paul's life?

8. What motivates him to keep pressing on toward the goal?

9. Based on Paul's words here and previously in Philippians, how would you define Christian maturity?

Paul wants to head off any idea that once you have become a mature Christian you have "arrived" in the sense that there is no more traveling to do. He gently warns against a super-spiritual view of Christianity which imagines that the full life of the age to come can be had in the present, without waiting for the resurrection. Paul is quite clear that he has not arrived; nor has anyone else.

10. Paul kept pressing on toward maturity because Jesus had already grasped Paul and taken control of him (v. 12). In what areas of your life would you like Jesus to take hold of you?

All Paul's efforts after holiness, after the work of the gospel, after the eventual goal of resurrection, are not a matter of his unaided effort to do something that will make God pleased with him. They all take place within the context of God's grace: King Jesus has grasped hold of him, and all that he now does is a matter of responding in love to that firm hand on the shoulder.

11. How has God helped you toward maturity through difficult places?

PRAY

Thank the Lord for his firm hand on your shoulder and for the certainty of his love for you. Pray that you will never fall back into trying to accumulate credits with God, but will continue to trust what Christ has done for you. Pray for those who are still hesitating to trust Christ for salvation.

NOTE ON PHILIPPIANS 3:2

Why does Paul call people "dogs" who are in this troublesome group? This is one of three ways Paul is turning their own words back on them. First, many Jews would refer to Gentile outsiders (who had not been circumcised) as "dogs." In the ancient world, dogs were mostly wild and verminous, not often family pets. No, he says, those of you who insist on ethnic purity for the people of God, you are the true outsiders, the ones who are actually unclean.

Second, the "bad works" people (or evildoers) is Paul's contemptuous name for the "good works" people. They are the ones who are insisting that only keeping the law will do as the standard for membership in God's people.

Third, he reverses the sneering accusation that Gentile Christians were not circumcised. Instead Paul calls Jews and Gentiles alike who worship God in spirit (as opposed to emphasizing the flesh) and who take their pride in King Jesus (as opposed to taking pride in family descent) the true circumcision.

NOTE ON PHILIPPIANS 3:14

Paul describes the prize waiting there at the finishing line with an interesting phrase: "the upward call of God in King Jesus" or "the upward call of God in Christ Jesus" (ESV). This has often been seen as simply "heaven," the place "up there" where Christians aim to go at the end, as the TNIV suggests with, "God has called me heavenward in Christ Jesus."

This can't be what Paul means, however. In verses 20 and 21, which we shall come to in the next section, he speaks not of our going up to heaven, but of the Lord, King Jesus himself, coming *from* heaven to earth, in order to transform the world and change our bodies so that they are like his own resurrected and glorified body. Living in "heaven" isn't the goal we are aiming at; rather it's living in God's new world with our new bodies. So the "upward call" seems to be the resurrection life itself. It means living in the present in light of that future.

7

CITIZENS OF HEAVEN

Philippians 3:17—4:9

Today the word *colony* is not exactly popular. It rings of the old days of imperialism. To have a colonial attitude is supposed to mean being patronizing, perhaps bullying, looking down on local people in far-off lands as an inferior species, good only to help increase the profits for the mother country back home. Philippi was a Roman colony. By the time Paul went there, it contained quite a number of families descended from the original Roman colonists as well as others who had benefited from the Roman presence—and a good many who hadn't and who resented the alien, Latin-speaking elite that had taken over their Greek town. All this is important if we are to understand this passage, which is in many ways the climax of Paul's letter to the Philippians.

OPEN

What does citizenship mean to you?

STUDY

1. *Read Philippians 3:17—4:1.* Paul boldly invites the Philippians to imitate his behavior (3:17). How have you been helped by the example of other believers?

2. What radical contrast does Paul draw between two different kinds of people?

3. Paul admits that he weeps at the behavior of people who are enemies of the cross (3:18). When have you been deeply affected by the actions of people who don't follow Christ?

4. What challenges does your church fellowship face from the world around you?

When Paul says "we are citizens of heaven," we naturally suppose he means "and so we're waiting until we can go and live in heaven where we belong." But that's not what he says, and it's certainly not what he means. If someone in Philippi said, "We are citizens of Rome," they wouldn't mean, "so we're looking forward to going to live there." Being a colony works the other way around. The task of the Roman citizen in a place like Philippi was to bring Roman culture and rule to northern Greece, to expand Roman influence there.

The church is at present a colony of heaven, with the responsibility (as we say in the Lord's Prayer) for bringing the life and rule of heaven to bear on earth. We are not very good at it. But our hope is that the true Savior, the true Lord, King Jesus himself, will come from heaven and change all that.

5. How will things be different when the Lord comes from heaven (3:20-21)?

6. What does Paul mean when he tells the Philippians to stand firm in the Lord (4:1)?

7. How has Paul himself already demonstrated this to them?

8. No doubt some in the Philippian church were Roman citizens and some were not. Regardless, Paul wants his readers to think out what it means to give their primary allegiance not to Rome but to heaven, not to Caesar but to Jesus.

    What would it mean for your church fellowship to live as a colony of heaven with the responsibility for bringing the life and rule of heaven to bear on earth?

9. *Read Philippians 4:2-9.* Verses 2-3 are a "special appeal" to two women in Philippi who are in conflict. Apparently the situation has been going on for some time, since Paul must have heard about it from Epaphroditus. No doubt he had this in mind when he wrote 2:1-4. When have you seen a dispute between Christians handled in a positive and healing manner?

10. In verse 4 Paul says to celebrate in the Lord. Often the word here is translated "rejoice." We normally understand that word today, I think, as meaning something that happens inside people, a sense of joy welling up and making them happy from within. All that is important, and is contained within Paul's command; but in his world and culture this "rejoice" would have meant what we would call a public celebration. How can we celebrate as Christians today?

11. In a polytheistic culture such as Philippi, why would many of the Philippians feel worried and anxious (see verse 6)?

12. How does verse 8 relate to Paul's discussion of conflict in the church found in verses 2-3?

13. Reflect on the promises of verses 7 and 9. How have you experienced the peace of God in the midst of difficult circumstances?

PRAY

Taking 4:6 as your model, pray about areas of life which you have considered too insignificant, or perhaps even too impossible, to bring to the Lord. As you pray, accept and claim the promise that God's peace will keep guard over your hearts and minds in King Jesus.

8

CONTENTMENT IN ALL CIRCUMSTANCES

Philippians 4:10-23

For Paul, the arrival of Epaphroditus was like spring flowers suddenly bursting into bloom, telling him the Easter message once more. Paul was quick to say as well that his deep gratitude for the money didn't mean he was the sort of person who would grumble or moan at God if he wasn't kept well supplied with creature comforts. On the contrary, God had put him through a tough school in which he had learned one of the most important lessons in life: contentment.

OPEN

What would you say is necessary for contentment?

STUDY

1. *Read Philippians 4:10-23.* Roman prisons didn't provide food for prisoners. That was left for friends and family. Now that Epaphroditus

has arrived, Paul has received the gift the Philippians had gathered for him (vv. 10, 18). How does Paul express his gratitude?

2. While expressing his thanks, how does Paul also distance himself from a complaining or grumbling attitude?

3. How do Paul's words and his attitude speak to a culture of discontent and cynicism?

4. In what ways do you find what Paul says to be challenging?

5. Paul would have struck many people as a human dynamo. His main public ministry probably lasted not much more than ten years, but he achieved more in that time than most people achieve in a long life. He suffered hardships and faced dangers that most people cannot even imagine. Why was he able to do it? Because of *the one who gives me power* (v. 13). He leaves it open as to whether *the one* means God or Jesus the Messiah, but it seems more likely that he

means God himself—the God, of course, whom we know in Jesus. In his letters Paul often speaks of the energy or power which he found welling up within himself, and which, as he declared, all came from God.

How have you found verse 13 to be true?

6. With whom have you entered or with whom could you enter into a partnership in suffering (v. 14)?

7. What motivates you to do this?

8. How had the Philippians turned out to be different from other churches Paul had started (vv. 15-16)?

9. Paul seeks to show gratitude while not letting anyone think he is really in this business for the money (v. 17). There were many wandering teachers and philosophers in the ancient world who would go from place to place selling their ideas, and many of them came to be regarded as crooks and cheats. So Paul returns to an accounting metaphor not to suggest for a moment that the Philippians were earning their salvation, but to say that God was delighted that their

faith, hope and love were finding this practical expression.

According to Paul, what blessings come from sacrificial giving (vv. 18-19)?

10. In verse 19 Paul made the Philippians a promise, not from himself but from God. How has that promise proved true for you?

At last we understand the full extent of why Paul is so grateful for the Philippian church's partnership in the gospel (see Philippians 1:5, 7; 4:14-15). It isn't just that they have sent him money with Epaphroditus as their willing messenger. It is that they have continued a habit which goes right back to the beginning. This is why the whole letter has the warm tone, the sense of deep trust and affection, that we have sensed throughout.

11. What practical help does this Scripture passage offer on being more grateful to God?

PRAY

Claim the promises of verses 13 and 19, not in a general way but for specific situations. Where do you need strength and renewed energy from God? How are you fearful about your needs not being met? What anxieties weigh you down? Pray about each concern, thanking God for the promises of verses 13 and 19 and their encouragement to you.

GUIDELINES FOR LEADERS

My grace is sufficient for you.
(2 Corinthians 12:9)

If leading a small group is something new for you, don't worry. These sessions are designed to flow naturally and be led easily. You may even find that the studies seem to lead themselves!

This study guide is flexible. You can use it with a variety of groups—students, professionals, coworkers, friends, neighborhood or church groups. Each study takes forty-five to sixty minutes in a group setting.

You don't need to be an expert on the Bible or a trained teacher to lead a small group. These guides are designed to facilitate a group's discussion, not a leader's presentation. Guiding group members to discover together what the Bible has to say and to listen together for God's guidance will help them remember much more than a lecture would.

There are some important facts to know about group dynamics and encouraging discussion. The suggestions listed below should equip you to effectively and enjoyably fulfill your role as leader.

PREPARING FOR THE STUDY

1. Ask God to help you understand and apply the passage in your own life. Unless this happens, you will not be prepared to lead others. Pray too for the various members of the group. Ask God to open

your hearts to the message of his Word and motivate you to action.

2. Read the introduction to the entire guide to get an overview of the topics that will be explored.

3. As you begin each study, read and reread the assigned Bible passage to familiarize yourself with it. This study guide is based on the For Everyone series on the New Testament (published by SPCK and Westminster John Knox). It will help you and the group if you have on hand a copy of the companion volume from the For Everyone series both for the translation of the passage found there and for further insight into the passage.

4. Carefully work through each question in the study. Spend time in meditation and reflection as you consider how to respond.

5. Write your thoughts and responses in the space provided in the study guide. This will help you to express your understanding of the passage clearly.

6. It may help to have a Bible dictionary handy. Use it to look up any unfamiliar words, names or places. The glossary at the end of each New Testament for Everyone commentary may likewise be helpful for keeping discussion moving.

7. Reflect seriously on how you need to apply the Scripture to your life. Remember that the group members will follow your lead in responding to the studies. They will not go any deeper than you do.

LEADING THE STUDY

1. At the beginning of your first time together, explain that these studies are meant to be discussions, not lectures. Encourage the members of the group to participate. However, do not put pressure on those who may be hesitant to speak—especially during the first few sessions.

2. Be sure that everyone in your group has a study guide. Encourage the group to prepare beforehand for each discussion by reading the introduction to the guide and by working through the questions in each study.

3. Begin each study on time. Open with prayer, asking God to help the group to understand and apply the passage.

4. Have a group member read aloud the introduction at the beginning of the discussion.

5. Discuss the "Open" question before the Bible passage is read. The "Open" question introduces the theme of the study and helps group members to begin to open up, and can reveal where our thoughts and feelings need to be transformed by Scripture. Reading the passage first will tend to color the honest reactions people would otherwise give—because they are, of course, supposed to think the way the Bible does. Encourage as many members as possible to respond to the "Open" question, and be ready to get the discussion going with your own response.

6. Have a group member read aloud the passage to be studied as indicated in the guide.

7. The study questions are designed to be read aloud just as they are written. You may, however, prefer to express them in your own words.

   There may be times when it is appropriate to deviate from the study guide. For example, a question may have already been answered. If so, move on to the next question. Or someone may raise an important question not covered in the guide. Take time to discuss it, but try to keep the group from going off on tangents.

8. Avoid answering your own questions. An eager group quickly becomes passive and silent if members think the leader will do most of the talking. If necessary repeat or rephrase the question until it is clearly understood, or refer to the commentary woven into the guide to clarify the context or meaning.

9. Don't be afraid of silence in response to the discussion questions. People may need time to think about the question before formulating their answers.

10. Don't be content with just one answer. Ask, "What do the rest of you think?" or "Anything else?" until several people have given answers to the question.

11. Try to be affirming whenever possible. Affirm participation. Never reject an answer; if it is clearly off-base, ask, "Which verse led you to that conclusion?" or again, "What do the rest of you think?"

12. Don't expect every answer to be addressed to you, even though this will probably happen at first. As group members become more at ease, they will begin to truly interact with each other. This is one sign of healthy discussion.

13. Don't be afraid of controversy. It can be very stimulating. If you don't resolve an issue completely, don't be frustrated. Explain that the group will move on and God may enlighten all of you in later sessions.

14. Periodically summarize what the group has said about the passage. This helps to draw together the various ideas mentioned and gives continuity to the study. But don't preach.

15. Conclude your time together with the prayer suggestion at the end of the study, adapting it to your group's particular needs as appropriate. Ask for God's help in following through on the applications you've identified.

16. End on time.

Many more suggestions and helps for studying a passage or guiding discussion can be found in *How to Lead a LifeGuide Bible Study* and *The Big Book on Small Groups* (both from InterVarsity Press/USA).

Other InterVarsity Press Resources from N. T. Wright

The Challenge of Jesus
N. T. Wright offers clarity and a full accounting of the facts of the life and teachings of Jesus, revealing how the Son of God was also solidly planted in first-century Palestine. *978-0-8308-2200-3, 202 pages, hardcover*

Resurrection
This 50-minute DVD confronts the most startling claim of Christianity—that Jesus rose from the dead. Shot on location in Israel, Greece and England, N. T. Wright presents the political, historical and theological issues of Jesus' day and today regarding this claim. Wright brings clarity and insight to one of the most profound mysteries in human history. Study guide included.
978-0-8308-3435-8, DVD

Evil and the Justice of God
N. T. Wright explores all aspects of evil and how it presents itself in society today. Fully grounded in the story of the Old and New Testaments, this presentation is provocative and hopeful; a fascinating analysis of and response to the fundamental question of evil and justice that faces believers.
978-0-8308-3398-6, 176 pages, hardcover

Evil
Filmed in Israel, South Africa and England, this 50-minute DVD confronts some of the major "evil" issues of our time—from tsunamis to AIDS—and puts them under the biblical spotlight. N. T. Wright says there is a solution to the problem of evil, if only we have the honesty and courage to name it and understand it for what it is. Study guide included. *978-0-8308-3434-1, DVD*

Justification: God's Plan and Paul's Vision
In this comprehensive account and defense of the crucial doctrine of justification, Wright also responds to critics who have challenged what has come to be called the New Perspective. Ultimately, he provides a chance for those in the middle of and on both sides of the debate to interact directly with his views and form their own conclusions. *978-0-8308-3863-9, 279 pages, hardcover*

Colossians and Philemon (Tyndale New Testament Commentary Series)
In Colossians, Paul presents Christ as "the firstborn over all creation," and appeals to his readers to seek a maturity found only in Christ. In Philemon, Paul appeals to a fellow believer to receive a runaway slave with love and forgiveness. In this volume N. T. Wright offers comment on both of these important books.
978-0-8308-4242-1, 199 pages, paperback